C000001469

He Still Heals

He Still Heals

Praying for a miracle with
three hours to live

Matthew Murray

New Life Publishing

New Life Publishing Co
Nottingham, England
First published in the UK 2017
Copyright Matthew Murray

ISBN 978-1-904835-03-5

Printed by Buxton Press, Palace Road,
Buxton, Derbyshire, SK17 6AE.

Cover image by Nick Jones

All rights reserved. No part of this publication
may be reproduced, stored in a retrieval system
or transmitted in any form or by any means,
electronic, mechanical, photocopying, recording
or otherwise, without the prior written
permission of the author.

FOREWORD

Matthew Murray knows what it means to pay the price for the sake of the gospel, to the point where he almost lost his life. His story is shaped and moulded by defining moments where God stepped in and literally saved him from the grips of death, so he can use that testimony, that moment of healing, that turning point, to set something greater into motion.

As someone who knows what sacrifice, sickness, and pain look like, I know where Matthew has been and what he's come through. I've been in full-time ministry for 50 years, 37 of those at Metro World Child in Brooklyn, New York.

Over the years, I've seen pastors and leaders give up, quit, and turn their backs on the ministry because of something they saw as a setback or something designed to make them fail.

In reality, it was an attack from the enemy attempting to stop the kingdom from advancing. Matthew's perseverance has pushed back against those attacks and God has proven faithful by restoring his health and opening doors that are truly amazing.

In my years of ministry experience, I've seen men and women come and go. Matthew is in it for life, because his life was given back to him.

Pastor Bill Wilson, Ph.D.
Metro World Child

This little book from Matthew Murray will bless your soul and increase your faith. Read it and give copies to your friends!

RT Kendall, author and teaching
pastor, Kensington Temple

You will be encouraged and inspired as you read the testimony of Matthew Murray. After being diagnosed with an aggressive form of malaria, his life was hanging in the balance. However, through the power of prayer from many around the world, God healed and restored his life. This miracle will strengthen your faith to believe that God is faithful and still heals those that call upon his name.

Evangelist Nathan Morris
Shake The Nations

If you ask me what Matthew Murray is equipped to do, I would say he starts stuff. That is an excellent quality in today's world. What this means is that he does not sit around depending on yesterday to catch up with him. If writing has ever come easy for anyone, it seems to come easy for Matthew. Have you ever noticed that bored people are boring and interesting people are interested? They seem to be interested in everything. Matthew is this kind of man and as you read this book you will see he captures his own story in a net, which is woven together in his words. You will recognise that his God-given skills are unclouded and shine brilliantly in each and every line he writes. His personal story is a story of the God who is with us now! I love you Matthew and believe in you always. And remember, healed people heal people.

Pastor Cleddie Keith
Heritage Christian Fellowship, Kentucky

When I heard that my friend Matthew Murray was seriously

sick in an American hospital and that it was actually life-threatening, we organised prayer on his behalf and began to battle in the heavens for his deliverance. What was remarkable is that I was scheduled to minister 45 minutes from his hospital bed and I had no Sunday night service – I knew that was a divine appointment that I could not miss. Matthew was in intensive care with all kinds of tubes inserted into his neck and he didn't look good. I knew I was there on assignment and I knew he would not die but be restored back to health. Well, as they say, the rest is history! God has healed him and he is doing what he loves; serving Jesus and building his kingdom.

Pastor Ken Gott
House of Prayer Europe

In this well-written and powerful book, Matthew Murray outlines the trauma of his near-death experience and the miraculous intervention of God that amazed everyone who witnessed it – including the medical profession. Rather than recoiling from future mission in the area, Matthew and his wife Becky – a great team – accelerate the work of 'One By One' that gives help and hope to thousands of the most vulnerable. The book is a great faith-builder.

John Glass, former General Superintendent
Elim Gospel Foursquare Alliance

Matthew's remarkable story of going from just a few hours to live, to miraculous recovery and ongoing ministry is such an inspiration. I love this man, his family and their passion to see the world changed for God. Read it and be inspired. Read it and know the same God is at work in your own life. Our God is still a miracle worker!

Jarrod Cooper, Senior Leader
Revive Church

During one session of prayer for Matthew I remember receiving the promise that 'what has happened to Matthew has actually served to advance the gospel' (Philippians 1:12). As we continued to pray, faith increased and everyone seemed to expect and believe for a full recovery. I remember announcing to the church that Matthew was healed and out of hospital and the whole church cheered. I can thank God that tens of thousands today have indeed heard of God's goodness through Matthew's story.

Pastor Dave Jones
Royston Bethel Church

The contents of this book are not the product of an overactive imagination, but a faithful and factual recollection of a series of amazing events! God is still healing people today, and Matthew Murray's story is living proof. As you read this book I pray that your faith will be ignited and your hope restored... mine was!

Doug Williams, Senior Minister
Emmanuel Christian Church, London

When you read this book, you will encounter a real, practical healing story through answered prayers of the saints of God. Whilst reading this book I came to tears knowing Matthew had only three hours to live and all human efforts were lost. This book has touched my heart and it has given me an increased level of compassion, hope and faith. Please read this real-life impactful book and see that against all odds, God will rescue you.

Nick Chanda
Redeemed Church of God Assistant Area Pastor &
Parish Pastor of Revival Christian Church of Enfield

I was enlisted to the 'Facebook prayer army' that Matthew's wife Becky initiated. As her husband's life was fast slipping away, Becky mustered faith and asked for others to do the same. Strangers prayed. I was one. Becky inspired us to hold on to God whilst hoping he would hold on to Matthew. Her faith was more potent than Matthew's malaria! Lean into this story and discover how God visited a hospital room and ushered in a miracle. Let this story fan faith in your heart from a tiny flicker to a blaze.

Helen Roberts
Wellspring Church, Watford

I'm glad Jesus made my daddy better.

Josiah Murray, aged five

This is an extraordinary story. A young leader flat out in pursuing the call of God to preach and demonstrate the love of Christ to the nations, Matthew Murray was literally stopped in his tracks by catastrophic sickness. 'He Still Heals' is the gripping account of Matthew's total healing and restoration and of the renewed hope and purpose that flows from a personal encounter with God's healing power.

Chris Cartwright
General Superintendent, Elim

THE FINAL FEW HOURS

The intermittent sound of beeping hospital machinery was my only comfort as I prepared for my last few hours on earth. I could barely open my eyes, I had no idea where I was and it seemed as if my entire body was failing and could shut down at any second.

I've often been asked what it felt like to be so close to death. Well, it wasn't pretty. As a pastor, I've been at the bedside of Christian people in their final days. There's often a clear sense of peace and comfort, almost an assurance from heaven that their future is safe and that their time has come.

This felt nothing like that.

In fact, you could say it was quite the opposite. The presence in my hospital room that day was dark, evil and scary. Lies would flash through my deteriorating mind and convince me that this was it. I'd drift in and out of consciousness as pictures of my little three-year-old boy, Josiah, would flick through my imagination. I'd never see him grow up. I'd miss his first day at school, his debut football match. He'd lack a father figure during his important teenage years and I wouldn't be there for his wedding. The pain was so intense that I didn't even have the strength to weep.

My gloomy thoughts then turned to my family in England. My precious parents who had stuck by me and supported me come what may. What must my mother be thinking? She's a worrier at the best of times, but this could be tipping her over the edge. Dad isn't the most emotional of characters. How would he be reacting? Would they even be aware of the situation? I panicked, wishing I could hear their voices just one more time.

Then a moment of genius struck... or so I thought. I mustered the strength to open my eyes and spotted a video camera stuck to the ceiling of my hospital room. Perhaps I could send my parents and close relatives a short greeting that they could play at my funeral and keep as a memory. What a smart idea...

I could barely speak, yet dug into the depths of my being to find my voice. I began to groan out my final message:

"Becky, I love you. Josiah, I'm so sorry you aren't going to have a daddy. Mum, dad... you've been the best. I'm sorry I won't be there for you. Please don't forget me."

The emotion then got too much. I burst out crying violently, so loud that a frightened nurse ran into my room and asked what was going on. She explained that the camera wasn't recording. What I had done couldn't be used as a video message for my loved ones – it was simply a CCTV camera monitoring my room. I felt devastated, confused and alone. The brief thought of contact with my family had been destroyed and the high doses of medication were messing with my brain.

To put it bluntly, I was terrified.

"You must have had lots of faith?" is one popular question I get asked. Let me be honest – it seemed as if I had none. No belief, no hope, no care and no future. This was it. At 27 years of age my time had come and it would only be a matter of minutes before the breathing would get harder, the beeping machinery would sound more urgent and I'd cruelly and suddenly slip into eternity.

"Did you ask God why?" is another favourite. No, not at

all. People much holier, better and more successful than me have seen their lives ended early. What about the babies in Africa who die of HIV? Or the innocent lives robbed at 9/11? I never quizzed God, complained to him or grumbled that I'd been dealt a rough deal. I simply gave up; it seemed as if I had no alternative.

Anyone reading this book obviously knows that the story has a much happier ending. It's taken me two years to even begin to write these words because I was so reluctant. I didn't want to be accused of marketing a miracle or hyping up a story that some will simply put down to good medicine or fate having its hand.

But as I've travelled telling this story and been interviewed by the media, whether in Europe, Africa or North America, I've learned one thing – people lack hope. Everywhere I turn there are men and women, irrespective of their race, wealth, status, background or religious view, who have little or no belief. Like me, they have given up. They've assumed the worst and have accepted defeat.

The Church hasn't always had the answers. "Where's your faith?" we've asked sorry congregants who have failed to get out of their wheelchairs. "You're obviously doing something wrong," we've blasted at parents whose children have turned their backs on God. We've somehow blamed others for a lack of miracles instead of looking to the sovereignty of God. We've moaned, complained and destroyed any remaining mustard seeds of faith that might have lingered in the hearts of desperate believers.

This book is meant to be easy to read, simple and real. There will be better and slicker titles you can turn to if you're looking for a deep and meaningful theological argument about Christ's healing power. I don't have all the answers. I'm just a simple example of God's grace and mercy. It's often said that 'healed people heal people' and my prayer is that this story will encourage you, lift your faith and give you the glimmer of hope you've needed to show you that God can turn your situation around.

Like Gideon of old, you might be asking: "Where are the miracles that our fathers told us about?" Well, there's one right here. I'm living proof that God still performs miracles, he still moves in response to prayer and he still heals.

Chapter 1

A TASTE OF AFRICA

"I've hardly noticed a mosquito all week," I famously told my friends as I returned from a thrilling mission trip to Kenya in September 2014.

Africa had held a special place in my heart for the best part of a decade. I went there as a new convert in 2006 and was instantly smitten. The smiles, the scenery and the simplicity of Africa and its precious people were things I could never forget. I longed to spend as much time on this continent as possible.

I'd been a Christian for just one year when I accompanied Nathan Morris, an evangelist and close friend, to Sierra Leone where we would later hold large gospel campaigns. Although I felt completely under-qualified to be Shake The Nations' crusade director, I fulfilled that role for several years. Nathan and I travelled the world together – it was truly a baptism of fire that changed me forever.

Having used all of my annual holiday allowance (I was a sports journalist for my local newspaper) for mission trips, I was presented with an opportunity to accompany Nathan to the rural village of Bumala B, Kenya, for his final mission trip of 2006. I asked my boss for unpaid leave and was instantly refused. I then made one of the craziest decisions of my life having attended a service led by American pastor Bill Wilson, who leads the largest Sunday school in the world based out of New York City. Pastor Bill challenged me on that cold evening in Rotherham to the extent that I handed in my notice at work the following Monday morning. I was throwing away my entire journalism career to be part of that one-week mission to Kenya. Well-meaning Christians tried to talk, counsel and pray me out of it, but my mind was made up. I wanted to serve Jesus – and nothing else mattered.

A few weeks later I was on a plane to Bumala B, and making the 24-hour journey wondering if I'd made the right decision. We were the first missionaries to visit this village, and locals were so sceptical that they nicknamed our campaign 'Mission Impossible'. What happened next was historic. Hundreds were converted, indisputable miracles took place and we planted the village's first evangelical church. Tribal leaders were so in awe that they documented the event in their history books, writing of the time the 'Living God' visited their village.

Fast forward a few years and today my wife Becky and I are the founders and directors of One By One, a missions organisation that runs King's Children's Home and School in that very same village. We reach approximately 10,000 children every week through schools outreach, have planted a further three churches and employ almost 40 staff. About 200 children are on our campus every day, and we are in the legal process of adopting those who are total orphans. It's said that big doors open on small hinges. We can testify to that!

As a journalist and now church pastor, I only make it to Kenya once or twice a year, but each visit is so precious. The children call me 'Daddy' and regularly write letters to me. Once abandoned, tortured and abused, these boys and girls are now born again and looking forward to exciting futures serving Christ. Whereas at one time they would dream of their next meal, they now aspire to be doctors, pilots and politicians. What a God we serve!

My role with One By One is simple. I get a lot of credit and pats on the back, but the truth is that I'm simply an overseer of a great team, spearheaded by Becky who has carried a heart for orphaned children since she was a young girl herself. The staff and volunteers are focused on rescuing and raising needy children who will eventually become the movers and shakers across Kenya. As Bill Wilson says: "It's better to build boys and girls than fix men and women."

On one particular trip in 2014 – my last before becoming the pastor at Renew Church, Uttoxeter – our team joked that the mosquitoes seemed quiet that week and must be in hiding. As usual, I hadn't taken any malaria medication – a foolish practice in hindsight, but one that hadn't failed me on my previous 20 or so mission trips to the Third World. I genuinely believed that God would protect me, so medication was pointless. Some would call it faith, others naivety.

Arriving back in England, I had a three-day gap before immediately taking another trip to the States, where I would be speaking in several churches and at a glitzy One By One fundraising banquet that had been arranged in Mobile, Alabama. We have to send tens of thousands of pounds to Kenya and now Sri Lanka each year, so these events are vital as children are sponsored and cash is donated to fund the ongoing ministry.

A few days into my USA trip, I started to feel weak throughout my whole body. I tried to run a couple of miles one afternoon but felt so ill I abandoned the exercise and went to bed. I put it down to exhaustion and jet lag. The thought of a more serious sickness didn't even cross my mind.

But the following day things worsened. I was speaking that Sunday morning for my friend Jeremy Moore at New

Life Church in Cincinnati, Ohio. I woke up feeling too sick to preach, but being a stubborn Yorkshireman, I soldiered on. Almost miraculously, the pain lifted during the service and we had a memorable time in God's presence. But immediately afterwards I was shaking, shivering and sweating during the car journey back to the house where I was staying.

That night, I felt concerned for the first time that this might be something more serious than a bout of flu. My host Vernel Perry offered me some basic medication which I accepted, hoping I'd wake up the following morning fit and well and ready for my flight to Alabama.

I still refused to give much thought to this worsening sickness. I knew God would take care of me – I figured that he'd never let me down in my previous decade of travelling the world and he wasn't about to start now.

Healing was something I very much believed in – as a child I was healed of a stammer that had led to me being bullied in school. I saw speech specialists who had no answers but, following a time of prayer and fasting by my mother, one day I recovered and suddenly started talking perfectly. As my mother jokes, I haven't stopped talking since!

Years later in 2010, Becky and I accompanied Nathan Morris to a two-day conference at Church of His Presence in Daphne, Alabama, which evolved into the hugely popular Bay of the Holy Spirit Revival. We were only supposed to stay there for a few days, but due to the outbreak of healings we stayed for almost a year as hungry believers flocked from across the world to witness what God was doing. That's worth another book in itself.

During this incredible outpouring, we witnessed a paralysed lady get out of a wheelchair and walk for the first time in more than 22 years, and a young boy's brain tumour disappeared after prayer. There were many other miracles, too. This was an exciting, inspiring and phenomenal part of our journey, and one that reinforced our belief that God still performs miracles today.

So whether it be a cancerous tumour, paralysis of the legs or the extreme flu-like symptoms I was experiencing on my flight to Alabama, I wasn't particularly worried. I knew that God had called me and equipped me and that I didn't need to worry. It might seem like a cliché, but I honestly believed I was safe in his hands.

Chapter 2

EBOLA ISOLATION

Have you ever met someone and within seconds come to the realisation that God has sent them into your life? That's exactly how I felt when I staggered into the office of Dr Mike Mahoney, of Eastern Shore Urgent Care in Daphne, Alabama.

Dr Mahoney took one look at me and knew something was wrong. I could barely stand, gripping the medical bed in his office tightly as I muttered my predicament with sweat dripping down my brow. I'd paid $100 simply to see Dr Mahoney – a huge surprise to this naive Brit who had grown up with the UK's freely available National Health Service.

Whereas some US medics are accused of taking advantage of patients for financial gain, Dr Mahoney was nothing of the sort. In fact, he handed me back my $100 and said he didn't want to charge me – a miracle in itself according to my American friends! Dr Mahoney was a Spirit-filled Catholic medical missionary who regularly visited poverty-stricken nations, helping the poor and offering medical aid. He'd heard about my sickness from a mutual friend and had a heart to help.

"Matthew, you're very sick," Dr Mahoney told me in his unforgettably sweet southern accent. "I'm going to give you some medication. If you don't improve within two days, you must come back and we may have to send you to hospital."

Coincidentally, that same week there had been worldwide chaos and panic following the outbreak of Ebola in West Africa. Although I had been on the east side of the continent, thousands of miles away in Kenya, alarm bells were ringing as different theories were discussed because the violent and deadly disease was spreading quickly.

I refused to overthink things though and, as positive as ever, assumed my illness would pass after Dr Mahoney's simple prescription of tablets.

Much to my surprise, however, the medication made no difference at all, and my condition quickly worsened. I became too weak to get out of bed, I had no appetite for food and I could barely speak. My wife Becky, a trained nurse, was also starting to become concerned, as were my friends Nick and Chelsea Jones who we were staying with.

Our fundraising banquet was drawing near and Becky, Nick and Chelsea were all systems go preparing for it. I was one of the keynote speakers and insisted that I'd be fit to attend, but plans were already being made should I not be able to. I had never cancelled a speaking engagement in my life, and I was determined that this important event wouldn't be the first occasion.

As the day of the fundraiser came around, I was too sick even to get out of bed. My head pounded constantly like it had been the victim of ten rounds in the boxing ring, my legs were frail and unable to withstand any pressure, the rest of my body shook and dripped with sweat as I prayed, pleaded and cried out to God to alleviate the pain. I'd never felt so ill in my entire life. I'm not a drama queen and I'm never one for visits to the doctor – but I knew I needed help. For the first time I became quite scared that this wasn't something normal, especially as the prescribed medication was having zero impact.

Stumbling into Dr Mahoney's surgery for a second time, and behaving like a 90-year-old dying patient in the way I dragged my feet along the floor, I collapsed in a heap in the doctor's office. I noticed the understandable panic on the experienced medic's face as Dr Mahoney picked up his phone and called the nearby Thomas Hospital, begging Becky to get me there fast. He said we didn't even have time to go home for our belongings. We should go straight there.

The huge car park at Thomas Hospital wasn't something I could brave, so Becky kindly dropped me off at the door and I hobbled towards reception.

"My name's Matthew Murray, you should be expecting me," I somehow blurted out in my weakening British accent. The receptionist seemed concerned. I clung to the desk knowing it was only that which was propping me up, but eventually I gave in, fell to my knees and began to vomit violently. Panic seemed to fill the air as doctors and nurses appeared out of nowhere. I was placed into a wheelchair, frantically rushed down a corridor and bombarded with a series of questions, all of which I was too weak to answer.

"Have you been to Africa recently?" panicked one doctor.

"Do we know what's wrong?" screamed a nurse.

"He has all the symptoms of Ebola," another stated, just loud enough for me to hear.

The word 'Ebola' hit me like a ton of bricks. The pain in my exploding head was temporarily forgotten about. I regained sanity for a split second and began to process what I was hearing. I could feel myself slipping, getting weaker and weaker. I was terrified, fearful, exhausted and in agony. Could this infamous disease that was killing thousands of people across the world have struck me? These doctors aren't stupid. They don't overreact. Yet I could see the fear on their faces. They looked helpless, out of control and terrified. This horrific monster that I'd read about in newspapers and watched on TV seemed awfully close.

I silently prayed, "God, help me!" It was about all I could muster. Becky soon arrived from the car, which was a huge comfort, but right now my brain had no time for sentiment. No medics were speaking to me; they had left Becky and I in a room and told her to wear specialised protective clothing. My head felt like it was exploding again, my body felt like it was shutting down and tears streamed down my face as Becky nervously yet lovingly gripped my hand.

It was then the doctor returned with the fateful words: "Mr Murray, we think you might have Ebola. We are going to have to quarantine you while we carry out some tests. We're very sorry."

Chapter 3

NOT ALONE

Tossing and turning violently, my mind was in a daze. I didn't know where I was or what I was doing, even who I was. I panicked that I wasn't at the One By One fundraising dinner, I had no idea where my wife, son and friends were, and the nurses – although very sweet and kind – were refusing to give me any information, despite my regular requests for updates on my worsening condition.

I did have my iPhone with me though, so in between the aggressive tremors that racked my body and the terrible waves of pain that coursed through me, I sent a few text messages to friends asking for prayer.

What seemed like hours passed before a doctor finally came to see me. She was donned from head to toe in protective gear and seemed scared even to look at me. It was strange being the object of someone's fear, but I could see the terror in her eyes as she stuttered an explanation of what might be wrong.

"Matthew, I know this isn't nice to hear but... erm, well, there's a good chance you might have Ebola. You have every symptom, and you were just in Africa last week," she said. My heart sank.

"We won't find out the results for a few days," she continued. "We can keep you monitored and ensure you're safe.

Also, we have tested you for numerous other diseases and we can confirm you have malaria."

"Malaria!?" I actually laughed. "Doctor, with respect, I meet children with malaria on every trip to Africa. We give them a few tablets, and within days they're running around playing football and games with the rest of the kids. This will be nothing. I'll be completely fine."

She nervously smiled at my naivety, carefully trying to explain that there were four different strains of malaria – I had the worst one. She warned me that my body wouldn't respond to the disease like a native African would and that it could take some time for me to recover.

I managed to call England to notify my parents of what was wrong and asked them to start praying. It was comforting to hear their voices, even though the phone call only lasted a few seconds due to my failing strength. In fact, it was so exhausting that I fell into a deep sleep soon afterwards.

A couple of hours later, I thought I was dreaming when I heard the cry of 'DADDY! DADDY!' in the distance. It sounded just like my little son Josiah, so you can imagine my joy as I opened my eyes and saw his face smiling at me. I gestured for him and Becky to come into the room and was confused when they continued standing behind the glass window looking in. Josiah looked excited to see me but the picture on Becky's face wasn't quite as jovial. She had a brave smile but I knew it was just that. Behind the grin was a face that screamed panic and fear.

She then pointed to her phone and told me to read my messages. I quickly looked for my iPhone and a fresh dose of trepidation and dread suddenly came upon me. I was deemed a risk to public health due to the possibility of having Ebola, and Becky and Josiah weren't allowed into my hospital room. I felt so deflated. The temporary joy of seeing Josiah's face and hearing his voice vanished in a heartbeat after finding out I couldn't even hold his hand. They had to wave at me from the window and blow kisses. It had been a long day for them – Becky had been with me in the hospital before going to speak at the fundraising dinner.

The pain of being alone overshadowed any headache or body tremors. It was terrifying to think I couldn't even hold my loved ones' hands in the darkest hour of my life. My wife couldn't run her fingers down my face and tell me everything would be OK. My little boy wasn't allowed to play games and climb into my bed and tickle me, my friends couldn't enter the room and take my mind off things by telling funny jokes. If there's one thing worse than suffering, it's suffering alone. I found that out the hard way.

As Becky and Josiah blew their final kisses and wandered off down the corridor, little did I know that it would be the last time I would see my adorable son for three weeks. I waited until they'd left before bursting into tears. I didn't want them to know how serious this was. I didn't want them to worry about my feelings as well as my physical condition. If I could put on a brave face, at least it would ease things, or so I thought. I sobbed and sobbed like a baby until my pillow was soaking wet.

However, it was in the midst of these tears that a beautiful truth hit me. Although I could have no physical contact with humans and was being treated as some sort of leper by the hospital system, it dawned on me that I wasn't alone in that isolation room. As a Christian and firm believer in Christ, I remembered the famous words that our Lord had promised never to leave us or forsake us. No quarantined room could hold back the presence of Almighty God. He was with me!

I didn't have the strength to pick up my Bible and begin to study the Scriptures, nor could I find the courage to enter a time of prayer and worship, but in the lonely isolation unit of Thomas Hospital, Daphne, Alabama, on October 2, 2014, I knew beyond a shadow of a doubt that I wasn't alone. And of that, I could be certain.

Chapter 4

THREE HOURS TO LIVE

Plasmodium falciparum is the most brutal form of malaria and kills more people every year than any other disease. If your bloodstream contains just five per cent of this evil parasite, you can be dead. If left untreated, it can spread to your organs like wildfire, quickly attacking the lungs, heart, liver, kidneys and brain until your entire body shuts down. It's a slow, agonising and painful deterioration. Few people ever survive such multi-organ failure.

On October 2, 2014, 20 per cent of my bloodstream was filled with this parasite – a whopping four times above the fatality risk rate. Soldiering on, unaware that I even had malaria, my condition had been left untreated for weeks, and my body was now rejecting all the medical assistance offered by the staff at Thomas Hospital.

I have little recollection of the days that followed. Becky – faithfully supported by our friends Nick and Chelsea – spent every minute she could at the hospital. Little Josiah simply couldn't understand what was happening. Despite lots of prayer, hope and faith, my condition only worsened.

Finally, on October 4, doctors pulled Becky into a side room and told her that the malaria rate had now spread to 50 per cent of my blood – the medication wasn't working and my body wasn't responding. I was somehow still breathing without the assistance of a ventilator, but I couldn't move, talk or even open my eyes.

"Your husband could be dead in the next two to three hours, Mrs Murray," the medics told my precious wife. "There's nothing more we can do. Every one of Matthew's major organs is affected and they're all getting worse. We're very sorry."

Becky tells me she immediately went into panic, howling out in tears as the reality of the doctor's words sank in. Her friend Chelsea held her and rocked her, tightly gripping her hands and praying that somehow God would intervene.

How would she break the news to Josiah? How would she telephone England to inform my parents? How would she cope with being a widow in her early 30s? What about the work in Kenya? She couldn't run it alone. These very real thoughts raced through her brain as she contemplated life without me.

Thankfully, I had no idea of the seriousness of the situation. I never heard that terrifying diagnosis or sensed the panic of my loved ones. I was spaced out, and had little grasp of anything, let alone the near-death experience my battered body was enduring.

Occasionally I would open my eyes. I'd hear the machines beeping and smile at a helpful nurse. I'd search desperately for Becky, being comforted when she was there and terrified when she wasn't. I'd grunt the occasional greeting or blurt out the odd confused sentence. At one point I became convinced I was in Atlanta, and that a church in North Yorkshire had come to visit me. Later I asked Becky if she had written the lyrics to the classic hymn Amazing Grace that she'd sung over me. To say I was confused would be an understatement.

I do, however, recall the sheer darkness that I experienced in my hospital room. I knew this was a desperate situation and that I was fighting for my life. I'd have occasional glimpses of my family, I'd think back to my childhood and recall early memories. It seemed as if my entire life was flashing before me.

I grew up in South Yorkshire in an area severely impacted by the Miners' Strike, a long-running and bitter dispute between the nation's coal miners and the Government. I'd grown up hearing stories of how men had to fight for their lives following the sweeping pit closures, and I knew that hard work and determination would be needed if I was to stay in this battle. There were times when I'd grit my teeth, remembering the men who had gone before me and survived against all the odds. If they could survive, perhaps I'd have a chance. Looking back it seems strange to draw on such unusual inspiration, yet those thoughts helped me during my toughest times.

The Bible says the devil comes to 'steal, kill and destroy', and although I'm careful with my choice of words when it comes to spiritual battles, it certainly seemed that something beyond human control was fighting against me. Slipping in and out of consciousness in the lonely hours of the night, I seemed to feel the devil's breath down my neck. "You're over," he'd whisper in my ear in that evil slippery tone. "Nooooooo!" I'd scream out. "Jesus save me!" The battle was real.

One night during an imaginary argument with my next-door neighbour, I felt my strength breaking. I screamed out for help, mustering up all the courage I had from the depths of my being. Becky and the nurses rushed in but no one could offer the comfort and healing that I needed. I knew I was being defeated and that time was running out. Becky's face told me all I needed to know. She looked helpless and although heavily confused by the high doses of medication I was receiving, I sensed enough to know that this war was coming to a close. It was a matter of life and death and it seemed as if I was losing.

There was also an ongoing battle between my friends and

family and the staff at Thomas Hospital who refused to rule out that I had Ebola. Malaria was clearly destroying my organs yet the results from the tests for Ebola still hadn't been returned. America, the land of lawsuits and controversy, couldn't take the risk that this infected Brit was Ebola-free, and the hospital chiefs insisted I remain in isolation. This made matters worse.

Becky and Nick would don the huge medical suits and masks as they would enter my room just to be with me for a few minutes. Mobile phones were banned yet Nick – ever the risk-taker and rule-breaker – sneaked in his iPhone one day to make a crucial call. He had been the Media Director at the Bay of the Holy Spirit Revival and knew all too well about God's healing power. After the medical staff had disappeared, he whipped out his phone, laid it on my chest and called Nathan Morris who began to pray over me. Nick tells me that although unconscious and silent, I responded to Nathan's familiar voice and actually muttered a sentence in tongues for a few seconds. Although I have no recollection of this, I'm comforted to know that the Holy Spirit was speaking through me even in my darkest hour.

FAMILY REUNION:
Reunited with my wife,
Becky, and son, Josiah,
who I hadn't seen for
three weeks.

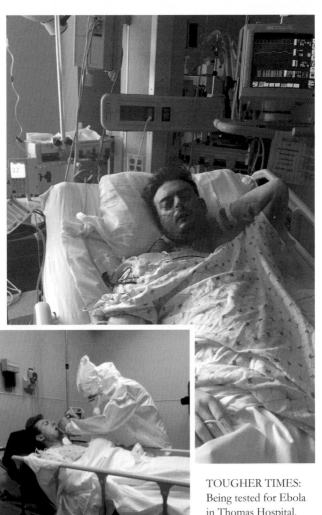

TOUGHER TIMES:
Being tested for Ebola
in Thomas Hospital,
Alabama, (left), and
(above), at the height
of my ordeal when my
organs shut down.

SUPPORT: I'll be forever grateful for the friendship and care of Brad and Carla Custis (top) and Nick and Chelsea Jones (middle), not to mention Becky and Josiah, of course.

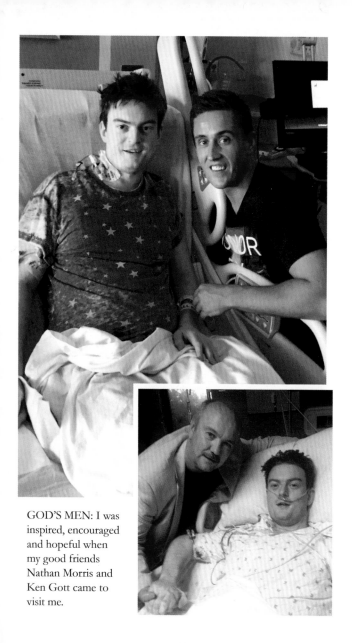

GOD'S MEN: I was inspired, encouraged and hopeful when my good friends Nathan Morris and Ken Gott came to visit me.

TRANSFORMED: The #Pray4Matt Facebook graphic that went viral, Pastor Cleddie Keith in London the day after I returned to the UK, and Dr Mike Mahoney, who treated me with true Christian care and compassion and has since become a good friend.

For all your motoring needs

WEEKLY VAN HIRE
FORD TRANSIT

£204.62 week

Derby Road, Uttoxeter
01889 563448

Pastor thanks the Lord for beating deadly bug

New minister makes miraculous recovery from malaria

POWER OF PRAYER . . . Matthew Murray suffered organ failure while he battled malaria, above, and, left, in full health with Becky and son Josiah.

By Joanna Craig
joanna.craig@staffs-news.co.uk

'THE power of prayer saved my

Uttoxeter Pentecostal Church in January when he and his family move to the town.

Doctors told Matthew's wife Becky Murray there was nothing they could

---

MEDIA MAYHEM: On my return I was surprised with the media coverage by both the Christian and secular press.

MALARIA MIRACLE

Dad lives on despite a total organ failure

JOURNALIST SHOCKS DOCS AFTER REC

I thought I was going to die, but God had other ideas

There were moments when Matthew Murray didn't think he would see 2015 after a near death experience in October. He told New Life about his remarkable recovery...

healing was 'a miracle'

MIRACLE

PARASITE

'I love a doctor or nurse walk in just to congratulate me on surviving'

MILLIONS: Speaking on local TV in Alabama after the miracle, and the Rotherham Advertiser's rather dramatic headline. It's estimated more than one million people have heard the story through the media.

ROTHERHAM
Advertiser

Doors & Windows
• Online pricing
• No Salesmen!

November 7, 2014   80p   YOUR TOWN, YOUR PAPER   Serving South Yorkshire

WIN £50 OF 7 TESCO GIFT CARDS!

WIN CLOTHES SHOW LIVE TICKETS TO THE

It's Christmas FANTASTIC 12-PAGE PULL-OUT INSIDE...

Julie Kenny

'm ely ue

uld be iconic house as targets urchase restora- impor- chestne

I-listed ppen to action by the 15 resi- work- and ties all up by Wood- Trust

ation Her- new now

'BACK FROM THE DEAD'

Man says power of prayer saved his life after medics failed

by ANTONY CLAY

A MAN has been dubbed Lazarus by friends after coming back from the brink of death.

Matthew Murray believes his miraculous recovery from a lethal strain of malaria echoed that of the Biblical figure who

● Continued on page 6

GRAVELY ILL: Matthew Murray is treated in a hospital   TOGETHER AGAIN: Matthew, wife Becky and son

MEMORIES: I've kept all the media cuttings and my little note from Josiah, of course.

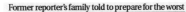

Former reporter's family told to prepare for the worst

'Mum, dad, I love you. This is it ... I'm dying'

By Mike Cotton

A FORMER Barnsley Chronicle sports reporter struck down by malaria was so convinced he was going to die he attempted to record a final message to his loved ones on a hospital CCTV camera.

Matthew Murray, 27, was kept in isolation in an American intensive care ward because doctors feared he had picked up ebola on a trip to Africa days earlier.

But he is now recovering well in America and believes a miracle saved his life after doctors told his wife there was nothing more they could do and to "prepare for the worst".

Matthew told the Chronicle from his Alabama hospital bed: "In my darkest moment I made a video message, saying 'mum, dad, I love you. This is it ... I'm dying'.

"I just saw this camera in my room and started talking – it turned out it was a CCTV camera and wasn't recording.

"But nobody was observing the footage at the time. I said a prayer to God before I went to sleep and when I woke up the doctors said it was a miracle I was still here.

Murray was reunited with his son Josiah after his spell in isolation while highly light have ebola when he was first admitted to hospital and denied NHS care to the risk of infection.

From few America on a orphanage, Alabama.

require disposable malaria tablets to make you ill and he had known people still get malaria despite taking them.

"It's been a really difficult side. My family took home in Barnsley have been very worried.

"The doctors all had masks and suits on, I had all the symptoms of ebola.

"My wife had to wear a mask to talk to me. But we're through the worst of it."

Matthew has had two spells working as a reporter, firstly in news in 2008 recently as a sports reporter.

He left in the summer to allow more time for his charity work.

Get Well Daddy

Chapter 5

FACEBOOK AND A CALL TO PRAYER

My wife Becky is an incredible woman of faith. I've seen her stand on the steps of mosques in Africa and fearlessly declare the name of Jesus. There have been times when she's gone into villages renowned for witchcraft, the occult and crime and boldly preached the gospel, seeing many respond and churches being subsequently planted.

She's a woman of miracles, love for Jesus, belief in God and – I'm extremely pleased to say – a woman of Facebook. I could have been accused of the occasional sceptical remark regarding social media prior to October 2014, but never again. In fact, you could say that Facebook helped save my life. Let me explain…

After receiving the news that I could be dead within three hours, Becky had a stroke of genius and posted an update about my health on Facebook. She knew it was desperate times and that our only hope was God. Have you ever been there? Have you ever had a situation where literally the only way out was through divine intervention? Perhaps you're going through one of those seasons right now. I pray that my story of hope will inspire you.

Becky nervously tapped the following few words into her iPhone that day: "URGENT: Please pray for Matthew. His body is not responding to the drugs. Please join us in prayer right now!!!" It was a simple, rushed, and panicky reaction, yet it was all what was needed to mobilise the most powerful army in world history to go to war.

It's often said that the Church is the hope of the world. The Bible describes the Church as the bride of Christ, and I saw firsthand this beautiful bride in all its glory, power, strength and victory. What I saw take place over the next few days was the most amazing demonstration of God's love and Christian unity that I've ever witnessed.

It's no secret that the Church has its faults. We've all been hurt by a pastor, an elder or a fellow believer at some point on our faith journey. But guess what... no one is perfect and we all make mistakes – even you! But let me say with full assurance, when it's on form, the Church of Jesus Christ is the most precious, loving, kind, generous and powerful army on the planet. When it gets over its disagreements, theological debates and pointless discussions, it really does have something to offer to a dying world. It certainly helped me on that day in October 2014.

I've always been fascinated by stories of prayer. One of my favourites is the account of the Hebridean Revival in Scotland when two old women cried out to God for the small island of Lewis and thousands came to Christ. I love the account in the book of Acts when Peter is in prison yet is freed after the Church remained in 'constant prayer'.

As Becky's desperate social media post – aided by our friend Nick's #Pray4Matt graphic – began to find its way across smartphones, laptops and electronic tablets across the world, we began to witness what Church is really all about. There was no bickering, backbiting or scandalous gossip, this was pure, kind and unified love. The Church stepped up and stepped in during my greatest hour of need and – I am convinced – saved my life through its persistent petition to heaven.

When you are given three hours to live, there's no time to call a prayer meeting or give advanced warning about a specific prayer rally. You have to pray – now!

In truth, Becky's message spread like wildfire. We'll never know quite how many people that Facebook post reached. It was shared hundreds of times, and thousands of comments began to flood in from all corners of the world as prayer networks, house groups and churches began to intercede.

As the Internet reacted, believers responded. News quickly spread to Sunderland in the north of England, where my good friends at Bethshan Church's 24-hour House of Prayer were meeting for their weekly gathering.

Luke Finch, the church's worship leader and son-in-law of senior pastors Ken and Lois Gott – heard of the situation, and he began to lead intercession during worship that night. Suddenly, lyrics began to spring forth from Luke's mouth: "Resurrection's in your veins, oh Matthew Murray. Resurrection's in your veins, so don't you worry." He repeated these phrases for more than 30 minutes as the precious saints in Sunderland went to war. Luke later told me that he specifically felt he should not pray for healing, but for resurrection.

Further afield, messages came in from Christians throughout the UK and America, Canada, Germany, Spain, France, India, China, Australia, New Zealand, Thailand, Colombia, Brazil, Argentina and various countries in Africa.

Becky would occasionally read me some of the messages and comments that had been sent, and tears would stream down my face as I learned how far-reaching this appeal had become. When she showed me the video of Luke singing and the Sunderland church praying, I sobbed like a newborn baby. It was no shock that my close friends and family were praying, but to see that this had spread to churches across the nations was humbling and overwhelming.

I must also mention the man I am proud to call my pastor, Cleddie Keith. Although I have never been a member of his church, Cleddie has pastored my family through many ups and downs over the years. And his church, Heritage Fellowship in Kentucky, has been one of our most consistent supporters of the work in Kenya. Cleddie is a veteran minister with a strong prophetic gifting, yet his tender and caring pastoral side came to the forefront when I was sick. He took two flights, hired a car and booked a hotel – probably spending well over $1,000 of his own money – to be with me and my family for three days. He wasn't even allowed into the room due to the Ebola scare, yet he held Becky's hand, comforted her, talked with doctors and mobilised his many friends to pray. My memory of his visit is vague, but I can briefly recall him entering my room for a few minutes and whispering the name 'Jesus' into my ear as he held my hand. I guess that's all I need to remember.

I later received messages from the General Superintendents of Elim and Assemblies of God, the two largest Pentecostal denominations in Britain. Both movements had sent out e-mails to their ministers asking for prayer and even took time out of the agenda of their National Leadership Team meetings to pray for my recovery.

I soon realised that this was far greater than one man's battle with malaria. This was a unifying of church streams, a breaking of denominational barriers and a coming together of Christians throughout the world in prayer to God. My view of the Church changed during this time. I now look beyond the faults, the flaws and the failings – this is God's bride we're talking about, the most incredible group of people on planet Earth.

Chapter 6

MALARIA MIRACLE

Three hours seemed like an eternity for Becky as she stared at my lifeless body. Although the Facebook feedback was exceptional and continued to be for many days to follow, she was still faced with the very real situation that her 27-year-old husband had been given just hours to live. A nervous-looking doctor then called her into a side room and her heart began to sink. Would this be the moment when all hope was abandoned and the fatal blow was delivered?

"Mrs Murray, we have some interesting news," the doctor said.

"In the last three hours, your husband's malaria count has gone from 50 per cent to 10 per cent and appears to be dropping."

My wife burst into tears. Just hours after asking believers across the world to pray, she was given this amazing and game-changing news. There had been no further medical intervention – my body had rejected the anti-malarial medication and proved to be allergic to the main treatment. There was no logical or natural explanation for this turnaround; it had to be God!

At this point in the story, many people wonder what the catch is. They assume there was some secret drug that produced the magic cure, or that the initial diagnosis was perhaps mistaken. It's natural for us to doubt and be sceptical, but I can assure you from the bottom of my heart that this was a genuine, bona fide miracle. I've told my story to health professionals across the world and every time they have been struck to silence. "There is no medical explanation for Matthew's recovery," said Dr Mike Mahoney when he read the report.

Despite the miracle news, my body wasn't instantly cured. I'd been to hell and back and my body had taken quite a beating, and I knew the fight was far from over.

"You're winning Matthew, don't give up," Becky told me one afternoon as I drifted in and out of sleep.

But I was extremely weak. I could hardly muster the strength to speak, and the gloomy events of the previous days had taken its toll on my battered and bruised body. I've maintained all along that I didn't have great faith, but perhaps I had just enough to get me through. I now needed to dig even deeper to fight through the next stage of this terrifying illness and begin my rehabilitation.

Although the disease was on its way out, my major organs were still affected. Cerebral malaria is no joke – it's ruthless with its victims and destroys vital body parts. If you do recover from this strain of illness, the implications can be life-changing. Permanent organ failure and lifelong brain damage are all very real possibilities.

One afternoon, forcing my eyes open to speak to a doctor, I was informed of my 'progress'.

"Matthew, your heart is enlarged, your lungs have collapsed and are functioning at less than 50 per cent, your liver is damaged and your kidneys will probably never work again without assistance. You might also have brain damage."

"Thanks doctor, now what's the bad news?" I joked, hoping humour would distract me from what I'd just been told.

Despite the negative diagnosis, at least for now we had

hope. The malaria was on its way out and doctors were speaking of my recovery, not my funeral. We still had a long way to go, but we had positive news. Facebook updates could resemble hope and faith rather than doom and gloom, and my precious family in the UK could finally get the news they'd been praying for.

During a deep sleep one Sunday evening in my intensive care room, I heard a familiar voice. I thought I must be daydreaming but I opened my eyes to find the unforgettable Ken Gott, a pastor from Sunderland, UK, in my hospital room.

"What on earth are you doing here?" I mumbled through the obstruction of the dangling oxygen tube.

Pastor Ken had been booked to speak at a church just 40 minutes from Thomas Hospital in Alabama. Midway through his conference he had a night off and was able to drive to see me. The story goes a little deeper. Ken and Lois had lost a son named Matthew who was stillborn some 27 years before. He would have been exactly the same age as me. When I met Ken and Lois in 2007, we realised that God had brought us together, and it's been a wonderful friendship ever since.

Pastor Ken is always jovial and is rarely seen without a smile on his face. God couldn't have sent a more suitable man into my hospital room that evening. He stayed for two hours, making us laugh with hilarious stories as I drifted in and out of sleep. He also showed his softer side as he fought to hold back tears seeing the state I was in. Although I believe God had already performed a miracle before Ken's visit, his appearance was significant. He cheered me up, and got me smiling for the first time in almost two weeks, and hearing a familiar British accent gave me a wonderful sense of home and family. I'll be forever grateful to Pastor Ken for taking the time to visit me.

Over the next few days, I felt strength coming back into my body. I was extremely weak, still unable to walk or use the bathroom without assistance, but I knew I was on the mend. Some days the pain would be so overwhelming as my organs were tested and examined by every expert Thomas Hospital had to offer. I'd have to grit my teeth and pray as minor setbacks would come, yet somehow I was filled with a peace that everything would be OK. The Bible says God can give us a peace that 'passes all understanding', and I strongly believe that was what my family and I were experiencing in Alabama. The diagnosis was still dire, the future still looked bleak, yet there remained an underlying hope, faith and belief that everything would turn out OK. What God had started, he would surely finish. I refused to believe that God had brought me back from the brink of death only to live with damaged organs – that's not the kind of miracle I was hoping for!

The malaria count rapidly went down to five per cent and then, eventually, it disappeared completely. To hear the medics tell me that the malaria had gone was such a relief. While there were any remnants of the disease in my blood I was filled with fear, so to get that news was another barrier that I felt I'd overcome.

I was then informed that my lungs were improving and I could breathe without oxygen, my liver had recovered and my heart was starting to function again. The number of tubes and machines were reducing and I even started to eat food – I had to survive on chocolate ice cream alone for the first few days of recovery as I discovered that every cloud has a silver lining!

I had three blood transfusions as the doctors attempted to get my organs working normally and I also started on dialysis to improve my kidneys, which were still in a severe and potentially life-threatening state. This would be the last remaining obstacle.

I look back on the malaria miracle with amazement. Not a day goes by where I don't think about it. It still baffles me that so many people prayed and that the parasite disappeared with no medical intervention. Even the experts were confused. This was more than a stroke of luck, a turn of fate or an answer to fine medical research. Believers prayed and God stepped in – that's the only explanation I can give. No one will ever convince me otherwise.

Jesus is still in the business of healing. It's rather simple really. The Jesus of the Bible went around healing the sick, and we are told that Jesus is the same yesterday, today and forever. If he did it then, why wouldn't he do it today?

Chapter 7

KIDNEY PUNCH

"Mr Murray, there's a good chance you'll be on dialysis for the rest of your life – and eventually you'll need a transplant. Your kidneys are almost at the point of total failure, and there's not much more we can do."

These were the brutal words of the renal specialist at Thomas Hospital as he explained the damage my body had endured during its near-fatal battle with malaria.

I had mixed emotions. On one hand I was thankful to be alive – just days earlier I had been face to face with death, so the very fact that I could speak and understand what the doctor was saying to me was a miracle. But on the other hand, I was a little bemused. Had God not healed me? Wasn't it as a result of prayer and petition that I had now recovered? Did the God who raised me from my deathbed only do half a job? Was I destined to a life of misery despite supposedly being healed? These were the questions racing through my confused brain.

One afternoon, I awoke to Becky's presence in my room and found myself muttering the words of Psalm 42: "Blessed is he who considers the poor, the Lord will deliver him in time of trouble…"

When reading the Bible, we cannot approach it like a normal textbook. But if we read it and allow the Holy Spirit to bring revelation, we will find ourselves captivated by its words. I had read the quoted Scripture a few years earlier and it had stuck with me. I believe the Holy Spirit brought it back to my memory at the appropriate time.

If you look after the poor, God will look after you. I've always believed that. There is something about ministry to the needy that attracts the Father's blessing. This, of course, shouldn't be our motive, but it should assure us that he will take care of us and be with us, even in life's fiery trials. I needed that assurance and a new wind of faith if I was to get over this latest hurdle.

Dialysis can be a cruel procedure. Typically used for older patients, it's tiring and extremely draining. In my case, the medics drilled a hole in my neck and attached a long tube to a 6ft-tall machine. They would hook me up to this machine for about five hours at a time. I couldn't talk, walk, eat or drink during the process; I simply had to sit there as excess fluid and waste products were drained from my blood – with the dialysis machine taking over the role normally performed by my kidneys. I was told I'd have to endure this for life, news that I found terrifying. At just 27 years of age, with my entire life ahead of me, how could I possibly spend five hours every day hooked up to this machine? It would kill off any travelling and overseas ambitions, that's for sure.

My heart began to sink. Josiah, my three-year-old son, still wasn't allowed to visit me and although the experts had now ruled out the Ebola scare and the staff's protective uniforms and masks were slowly disappearing, life was pretty low in that hospital room. I'll be honest – there were times when I wished it could all be over. I didn't have the stomach for another fight, and I often wondered if the world would be a better place without me. Suicidal thoughts – although not extreme – flashed through my mind as I tried to figure a way out.

By Friday of that week I was mentally and physically exhausted. I'd endured 25 hours of dialysis and thankfully the doctors told me that I could have the weekend off but would resume my treatment on Monday. My friend and former colleague Nathan Morris had told Becky that he and his wife Rachel would visit me that Sunday. I was delighted to tell my doctor of Nathan's visit, and quipped: "My friend who's a healing evangelist is coming to see me. I don't think I'll be needing that dialysis machine on Monday." Half joking and half speaking in faith, I laughed at the doctor's reaction. He must have thought the malaria had certainly gone to my brain as, to him, what I was saying was simply foolishness.

I must say a few words about Nathan Morris. He led me to Christ in 2005, baptised me, allowed me to preach my first sermon and took me on my first mission trip. I became his best friend, the best man at his wedding and we travelled the world together preaching the gospel. And although we aren't as close nowadays due to our geographical differences, he remains a close friend. When Nathan walked into my hospital room on October 19, 2014, I was instantly taken aback by the look in his eyes. Although he carried some treats (British chocolate was most welcome in my hour of need), bringing some grapes, flowers and a few caring words was not at the top of his agenda. He had what I can only describe as a fire in his eyes. There were few pleasantries. He simply said: "Matthew, God spoke to me. I had to be here. He said he is healing you and you will be discharged within one week."

Wow! Now we were talking! Forgetting suicidal thoughts and dark depression, the gift of faith immediately entered the room. I instantly believed that I would recover fully and there was not an ounce of doubt in my mind. My mindset and outlook changed completely in an instant.

Nathan's visit was enjoyable. We talked for hours and reminisced of our ventures together, and then he prayed a simple prayer. There was no spooky manifestation. I didn't tremble under the Spirit or fall to the floor (I was so weak that would have probably killed me) and I didn't speak in tongues. I simply agreed with him and said amen. There wasn't much else I could do! Nathan and Rachel hugged me, left their gifts and then drove back to Orlando, where they now reside. I later found out that Nathan had cancelled a large conference in the UK simply to visit me – I am humbled that he would do that. It was a reminder that in our pursuit of success we must always be willing to stop for the one. Nathan's visit was certainly a seminal moment in my recovery process.

The following day, at about 6am, the nurses came in to take some blood tests. I'd been pricked and poked every day for almost three weeks so I was quite accustomed to their treatment, but this time I was feeling a little different. I was so tired that Nathan's visit just the day before felt like a distant memory, but to my surprise the doctor came in two hours later and told me: "Matthew, there's been a significant improvement in your kidneys over the weekend. We'll give you one more day off the dialysis machine, but you'll be back on it tomorrow."

"Wow," I thought to myself. "Has God begun to do something?" I didn't allow myself to get too excited, but couldn't resist reminding the doctor of our earlier conversation.

Tuesday came around and I felt stronger still. The same thing happened and the doctor said there had been further improvement to my kidneys and that he'd give me one more day off the machine, but that I'd be back on it tomorrow. My faith was starting to increase. "Doctor, I don't think I'll be needing it again," I declared.

Then came Wednesday. Blood tests, reports, diagnosis. I was used to the system. And to my amazement, the doctor had more good news, although he still remained sceptical. "Matthew, I must admit that your kidneys are improving at a fast rate. I will give you one more day off the dialysis, but don't be shocked if you're back on it tomorrow!" I burst out laughing. "Doctor," I said. "Don't you see what's happened? Jesus is healing me!" We both laughed as he departed.

That afternoon there was a knock at my door. "Are you Matthew Murray?" a sweet lady said. "It depends who's asking," I replied. "Well, I'm one of the assistants. The doctor has sent me in here because he wants me to take this dialysis machine and use it on another patient. Is that OK?"

"Yes, yes, yes! Take it. Please!!!" I couldn't believe what I was hearing and then seeing as this ugly machine was wheeled out of my room.

And that's the last time I saw it. Ten days after being told I'd probably be on dialysis for life and even then need a kidney transplant, I was dialysis free and my kidneys were declared normal. Now all I needed was the all-clear to go home!

Chapter 8

DISCHARGED

You find out who your true friends are when you're going through a tough time. I discovered this during my hospital stint in Alabama. There were people who never messaged me who I thought would have been the first to my bedside, and yet acquaintances I barely knew showered godly love upon me and my family in beautiful ways.

I've already talked about Nick and Chelsea Jones who were absolute heroes to Becky and I, and another couple I'd like to mention is Brad and Carla Custis, who made the extraordinary 17-hour journey from Van Wert, Ohio, to visit me in Alabama. To a Brit who can drive the entire length of the British Isles in less time, that is truly astounding, and I am still humbled that they would come all that way to see me and send greetings from their precious church.

I first met Brad and Carla in 2009 on a mission trip to Kenya. We immediately became firm friends and several years later we invited Brad to join our USA board of directors. He remains one of my best friends, and exemplifies American loyalty and patriotism with near perfection.

It was perhaps fitting that the day after Brad and Carla arrived, I received the news we'd all been waiting for – I was being discharged from Thomas Hospital after 21 days of treatment. Nathan Morris had prophesied that my ordeal would be over within a week, and rather poignantly, it was just five days after he delivered the word that I finally left the hospital.

True to form, my exit wasn't without drama. As you can appreciate, there weren't too many British malaria sufferers who had been tested for Ebola in Alabama, so my story became quite well known amongst staff at Thomas Hospital. When word got around that I was leaving, doctors, nurses and hospital workers literally lined up to see me. It was surreal being the centre of such attention.

"We were here the night you were admitted. We all said in the staff room that we didn't think you'd make it," said one of the porters.

"The faith of the people around you has been inspiring. We are so glad you survived," said another worker.

Perhaps the best message came from one of the nurses: "Your recovery restored my faith in Jesus Christ," she told me on Facebook. Does it get any better than that?

I had lost almost 50lbs in my three weeks in hospital and my legs were so out of use that I struggled to walk. But as I was packing my belongings and getting ready to leave the hospital, the words of my friend Bruce Wagner flashed through my mind. Bruce, a businessman and long-term supporter of One By One, visited me when I was in intensive care. I remember very little about his visit, but I do recall him tightly gripping my hand and proclaiming: "You will walk out of here like a man."

As I bid farewell to the hospital staff who had become like friends, kissed the nurses who had cared for me with absolute professionalism, and stared for one last time at the walls that had seemed to imprison me for so long, Bruce's words wouldn't leave me. A sense of prophetic fulfilment came upon me and I told the porter who had brought a wheelchair to wheel me out of the hospital that I wanted to walk outside –

like a man! Forgive my ignorance, but I'd forgotten I was in America and didn't feel that such a request was so unreasonable, but I was reliably informed that in the land of lawsuits, walking out of hospital isn't as straightforward as I'd hoped so the wheelchair was my only option.

I briefly accepted this, but yards from the main double doors downstairs, I halted the porter in his tracks and insisted he let me get out of the chair. He reluctantly obeyed and, with no assistance whatsoever, I fulfilled Bruce's prophecy and stepped over the threshold of the hospital all by myself. Healed, restored, well and free, Matthew Murray had somehow made it into the big wide world!

What I didn't expect was the sudden emotion that would hit me. I flung my arms around Becky and wept like a newborn baby. The simplest of things would make me cry. I'd stare at the sky or admire the trees and would instantly become emotional and burst out in tears. I was grateful to be alive, and the wonder of God's creation seemed to overwhelm me. It sounds a bit sentimental looking back, but I was truly thankful for what God did. I shouldn't be here to tell this story, and yet I am. God kept me alive. He didn't have to lean down into that hospital and save me that day, but he did. And I never want to forget what he did for me.

The first night back at Nick and Chelsea's house was interesting. I hobbled up the stairs and just about made it to the bed. A bucket had been placed in my room in case of toilet emergencies and standing up was quite a challenge. It was clearly going to take some time for me to get my strength back. It took me quite a while to fall to sleep that night. I experienced sudden flashbacks of intensive care and would remember the darkness of just a few weeks ago. But eventually I drifted off into a deep sleep, and boy did I need it.

Chapter 9

VOICE TO THE NATIONS

Having worked in secular media for most of my life, the last thing I wanted to hear was a message saying I was about to return to that field. But that's exactly what happened when Tracy Stewart, a prophetess from North Carolina, e-mailed me and wrote: "The Lord says, 'I'm bringing his voice back into the secular realm. And he will be elevated as a voice across the nations, and this will come by no effort of his own.'"

I had never met Tracy Stewart at this point but had heard of her reputation as a powerful prophet. The e-mail she sent me was incredible. She named dates and seasons in my life that no one knew of. I was absolutely amazed, although the part about returning to the secular realm wasn't something I understood or desired.

But that same week, I received a phone call from a TV journalist named Pat Peterson, who worked for WKRG, an affiliate station of American TV giant CBS. He'd been tipped off about my Ebola scare, illness and subsequent recovery and said he'd like to come and interview me and broadcast it across the state. This was interesting. I was sceptical of his motives and concerned that they might try and discredit my Christian faith but, ever the risk-taker, I agreed. So it was that just a day after my release from hospital I was at a remote lake near Daphne, Alabama, being filmed, along with Becky, about my story.

I must say Mr Peterson was excellent. He was respectful of my beliefs and in no way mocked me when I proudly declared that Jesus Christ was the reason for my recovery. The interview was broadcast across Alabama and then went online. We estimate it was viewed almost 500,000 times.

We rented a beautiful condo at Orange Beach for a few days as a way to thank our friends Nick and Chelsea for their kindness and generosity, and a week or so after being discharged, we were finally on our way back to England. My body was extremely weak, I was sleeping a great deal, and I'd discovered I had a blood clot in my arm due to some of the medical procedures I'd endured. This set me back a few days but I was assured it would heal within a few months, which it did. Becky managed to plead with Delta to give me a business class upgrade, which they granted due to our special circumstances. This was just one more example of God's provision, which had been our experience throughout the entire ordeal.

Becky would visit me in hospital three times each day in the midst of looking after Josiah, but one afternoon she realised she'd forgotten her purse. Her car's fuel tank was almost on empty and she had no money for lunch. You can imagine her surprise when a complete stranger approached her and handed over $20, saying she'd been prompted to do so. This was utterly amazing and provided some food and fuel for the car. We regularly seek God for 'big' miracles, but the smaller ones are just as important. Remember, his eye is on the sparrow! No task is too big or too small for him. If it matters to you, it matters to him!

Another financial miracle came as I was leaving Mobile Airport. A businessman who asked to remain anonymous contacted me and said he'd like to wave us off before we departed for

England. He was aware that we'd been fundraising on our trip for our work in Kenya and had been forced to cancel speaking engagements due to my illness. As I stepped out of the car, he had a big beaming smile on his face as he handed me a piece of paper. "That's for you, son. Go and rescue some children and be blessed," he told me in his sweet southern accent. I folded the piece of paper up and didn't open it until I got through the terminal. You can guess my reaction when I saw that it was a cheque for $45,000. That kind of money goes a long way in Africa, and I even joked to Becky that I'd do another three weeks in hospital for that kind of payment!

On returning to England, the emotion was evident as I hugged my dad at Manchester Airport. He was overjoyed to see me and it was such a special moment. My mother had thought she would never see me again, and friends and family piled into the house in what became a very busy first 24 hours back in the UK.

It so happened that my American pastor, Cleddie Keith, was in London at the same time, holding a conference in Enfield with Pastor Nick Chanda, another close friend. I thought it would be a nice surprise for the team if I arrived for the final evening's service. I ignored all well-meaning counsel to stay at home and rest, and drove myself to London. When I pulled up at Enfield Baptist Church, where the conference was being held, Cleddie thought he was seeing a ghost! The last time he had seen me I was covered in tubes and on medication, so he was amazed when I jumped out of the car and gave him a giant squeeze. Of course I shared my testimony that evening to the joy of the exuberant and excited crowd.

It was fascinating to meet many friends and strangers who said they'd been praying for me. Natasha Chanda, Pastor Nick's eight-year-old daughter, told me she had seen a vision of me getting better. Peter Wreford, a close friend and publishing colleague, said: "Helen and I prayed for you like you were our own son." Peter had also been instrumental in mobilising the Elim Movement of churches to pray, and their General Superintendent John Glass had written to his ministers on three occasions asking for prayer and giving updates.

Having been checked out by a UK doctor and given the all-clear, I was free to give media interviews back home. The Rotherham Advertiser, our local newspaper, was the first on the scene, and the story also appeared in the Uttoxeter Advertiser, the Barnsley Chronicle and on BBC Radio Sheffield, amongst other secular outlets. Christian titles including iBelieve Magazine, New Life Newspaper, Direction Magazine and Good News Newspaper also covered the story as thousands upon thousands read and heard of God's healing power.

"Are you the guy who had malaria? We were praying for you!" said one man at the doctor's.

"Hey Matthew. You don't know us but we've been praying for you at our Bible college," said a young couple to Becky and I in a local restaurant.

I soon realised that this story had spread far and wide. It seemed that everyone I spoke to had heard of it and had been praying. Perhaps the most humorous media coverage came via the Daily Star, a tabloid read by half a million people a day in Great Britain. The paper is known for its celebrity gossip and half-nude images of models, so reporting on the healing power of Jesus isn't their usual modus operandi. But in fairness, they were proud and delighted to feature the headline 'MALARIA MIRACLE' and wrote: "Matthew Murray is one of the first in the world to survive multi-organ failure." I didn't quite have the Daily Star's boldness when I bought a copy of their paper for the first and only time in my life, furtively tucking it under my coat and hoping no one would see me with it!

Preaching invitations immediately rolled in and, within

a month of being back in Britain I'd already spoken in ten churches. To this day the momentum hasn't stopped or slowed down. Although I've tried my best to shake off the 'malaria man' tag, churches love the story and often invite me to speak at their evangelistic events. The story gives hopes to everyone, no matter where they are on their journey of faith.

Speaking at the Assemblies of God 2015 conference was a huge honour, and to share a pulpit with Nathan Morris in Rotherham was another privilege, as he interviewed me and asked me to tell the story. There have been many other memorable occasions and the list would be too long to print here.

With media interviews and speaking invitations to churches large and small, we estimate that more than a million people have now heard the story. It's staggering, exciting and humbling. And if there was a danger of pride creeping in, Pastor Cleddie soon put a stop to that: "Don't forget, all you did was nearly die," he once told me. Thanks Cleddie!

He Still Heals

Chapter 10

HE STILL HEALS

So far this book has been about my story. Of course, one of my intentions of writing it was to proclaim and testify to the miracle of healing I experienced. But now, what about you?

As I've travelled across the world telling this story, on every occasion without fail someone has approached me afterwards and asked for prayer. They've poured out their own problems and come to the conclusion that without God's miraculous intervention, they are finished.

My primary reason for putting this story into print was to show that even when you've been written off, there is always hope.

I was content with the story being available on YouTube and online and felt that publishing a book might appear showy and arrogant. But I've gotten over that and feel excited about the impact these words can have.

One of my biggest concerns with the healing movement in the Church is that such a great emphasis is placed upon the faith of the person who is sick. I unashamedly tell people that I had very little faith when I was in hospital – there were moments when I honestly thought I was about to die. And that's OK. God doesn't want us to be dishonest or put on some pretence that we're a superstar Christian with a perfect persona and no natural feelings.

In the story of the lame man who was lowered through the roof by his friends in front of Jesus, the Bible says it was because of 'their' faith that he was healed. The guy on the mat was probably terrified that his friends would drop him; perhaps he wasn't even thinking about a miracle! But his buddies were – they got him over the line and got him to Jesus. The pressure wasn't on him. In his hour of need, his faith-filled friends stood in the gap for him. I can resonate with that. Sometimes we need other people to fight for us. That's the power and the beauty of a unified Church.

Jesus says that faith as small as a mustard seed can move a mountain. Imagine how much faith you might need to see your bad back recover or for your migraine to disappear. It's not as much as you might think! You do need some faith because without faith it's impossible to please God, but you don't need a lot. You don't need to be the next Elijah or Moses to get a miracle from God. He can and will perform a miracle for you – you just have to find a tiny little bit of hope. It's attainable for everyone!

"Why does God heal some and not others?" It's a question I get asked all the time. I wish I had the answer, I really do. But I have to hold my hands up and say that I simply don't know. I remember a BBC journalist getting angry with me during one debate. "Do you think you're some kind of special creation that God chose to heal and yet he lets millions of children die of HIV?" It was tough and awkward, but I simply said I believed God healed me and couldn't account for other actions. It isn't a cop out and I'm not ducking the question; I simply don't have all the answers. Complicated theories and explanations can sometimes do more harm than good.

Despite the fact that not everyone is healed, I still believe in God's healing power. I've determined that I will always pray for the sick, always believe for miracles and always try to instil that faith into others. For me, it's much easier to believe God than to doubt him, and even when desperate parents line up asking for prayer for their cancer-riddled child, or when I'm called into a hospital and asked to pray for someone in a coma, I always believe the best and trust that God will come through. I'm pleased to report that there have been several testimonies of people being healed after hearing this story, along with dozens making decisions for Christ. This, of course, is always the greatest miracle.

Sickness and depression often come hand in hand. When you're ill, the temptation is to become depressed. I mentioned earlier that I even experienced suicidal thoughts in my darkest hours. That's not easy for a preacher to admit, but I now understand the complexity of sickness. It affects all areas of your life, not just the parts of your body that are directly impacted. Since being ill, my attitude to those who are sick has changed completely. I have a compassion and a love that I never had before. It's important that we don't judge people for being depressed – feeling trapped in an illness is extremely difficult.

Timing is also important. Not everyone is supposed to get healed TODAY despite what the TV evangelists might tell you. If it was that simple, why are people still being wheeled out of their meetings in wheelchairs? Timing is crucial to understanding healing. God chose to heal me three weeks into my ordeal. He could have done it sooner, but he knows all things and everything is perfect in his timing. I firmly believe that God will get glory out of every situation. If he had healed me instantly, I wouldn't have met the dozens of great medics who assisted me, not to mention the media and evangelism opportunities that wouldn't have arisen. God is able to make all things work together for his glory!

If you're going through a tough trial, whether it's a sickness, a relationship, a troubled son or daughter or even a financial worry, be assured that God will come through for you. He will provide peace in the midst of the storm and in his own perfect timing will give you your heart's desire. Following my malaria miracle I strongly believe that, and I'm praying for every reader of this book, that God will bring comfort and joy to your heart. Keep believing and never give up. Your miracle – just like mine – could be just around the corner.